LIVING WELL

EXERCISING
FOR GOOD HEALTH

By Shirley Wimbish Gray

THE CHILD'S WORLD®
CHANHASSEN, MINNESOTA

The
Child's
World®

Published in the United States of America by The Child's World®
P.O. Box 326, Chanhassen, MN 55317-0326
800-599-READ
www.childsworld.com

*Subject Consultant:
Diana Ruschhaupt,
Director of Programs,
Ruth Lilly Health
Education Center,
Indianapolis,
Indianapolis*

Photo Credits: Cover: Creatas; A. Ramey/PhotoEdit: 11 right, 23; Corbis: 5 (Reuters NewMedia Inc.), 9 (Strauss/Curtis), 16, 18 (Kimbell Art Museum), 19 (Pawel Libera), 20, 21 (Jim Erikson), 22 (Rick Gomez), 24, 25 (Richard Hutchings), 31; Custom Medical Stock Photo: 6; David Young-Wolff/PhotoEdit: 10, 14; PhotoEdit: 7 (Will Hart), 11 (Tony Freeman), 12 (Merritt Vincent), 13 (Cindy Charles), 17 (Bill Aron), 26 (Michael Newman), 27 (Richard Hutchings); Spencer Grant/PhotoEdit: 8, 21 right; U. S. Department of Agriculture: 15.

The Child's World®: Mary Berendes, Publishing Director

Editorial Directions, Inc.: E. Russell Primm, Editorial Director; Elizabeth K. Martin, Line Editor; Katie Marsico, Assistant Editor; Olivia Nellums, Editorial Assistant; Susan Hindman, Copy Editor; Sarah E. De Capua, Proofreader; Peter Garnham and Chris Simms, Fact Checkers; Tim Griffin/IndexServ, Indexer; Elizabeth K. Martin and Matthew Messbarger, Photo Researchers and Selectors

Library of Congress Cataloging-in-Publication Data
Gray, Shirley W.
  Exercising for good health / by Shirley W. Gray.
      p. cm. — (Living well)
Includes index.
Contents: Be your best!—What is physical fitness?—How can you get fit?—Why food matters—Why be active?—Get moving!
  ISBN 1-59296-081-2 (lib. bdg. : alk. paper)
  1. Exercise—Juvenile literature. 2. Children—Health and hygiene—Juvenile literature. 3. Physical fitness for children—Juvenile literature. 4. Exercise for children—Juvenile literature. [1. Exercise. 2. Physical fitness. 3. Health. 4. Nutrition.] I. Title. II. Series: Living well (Child's World (Firm))
  RA781.G785 2004
  613.7—dc21   2003006279

TABLE OF CONTENTS

CHAPTER ONE

Do Your Best!

When Nikki McCray was 13 years old, she decided she wanted to

play basketball with her older cousins. She started practicing every

afternoon after school. She gave it her best effort, and soon she was

playing for her school team.

Today, Nikki is still giving basketball her best effort. She plays for

the Indiana Fever in the WNBA. She knows that staying physically fit

is one way to do her best. Nikki runs to keep her heart healthy. She

also stretches her muscles and works to keep them strong.

Nikki has enough energy to do her best off the court, too. She

enjoys singing, and she volunteers in her community.

What do you enjoy doing? Maybe you like to play sports, like

Nikki. Or maybe you prefer to camp and hike. Lots of children enjoy dancing or playing in a band. Whatever you do, being physically fit

can help you do your best, like Nikki does.

Keeping physically fit helped Nikki McCray compete as a member
of the U.S. women's basketball team in the 2000 Summer Olympics.

WHAT IS PHYSICAL FITNESS?

Physical fitness means keeping your body healthy. When you are physically fit, you look and feel your best. You have the energy you need to work and play. You also feel good, so you do not get upset easily when little things go wrong.

People who are physically fit have strong hearts. The heart pumps oxygen and **nutrients** from food to all parts of the body. When you are active, you breathe harder

Being active keeps your heart pumping nutrients and oxygen all over your body.

and your heart beats faster.
Aerobic (air-OH-bic) exercise
causes your body to use more
oxygen. This strengthens your
heart and lungs. Running and
swimming are two terrific
ways to keep the heart and
lungs in shape.

*Lifting weights is one way
to help build strong muscles.*

Strong muscles are also a part of being fit. If you have strong

muscles, you can lift heavy things. Many athletes lift weights to

help them develop strong arm and back muscles.

As your muscles get stronger, you will also build endurance

(in-DUR-ans). You will be able to use your muscles for longer

and longer periods of time without getting tired. Do you know

You need strong stomach muscles to twirl a hula hoop for a long time.

someone who can do 20 sit-ups? How about someone who can twirl a hula hoop for 15 minutes? It takes strong stomach muscles and lots of endurance to do these activities!

Strength and endurance are two important parts of being fit. So is being flexible (FLECK-suh-bul). This means that your joints and muscles can bend and stretch easily. Flexible muscles are less likely to get hurt during an activity.

Try touching your toes to see if you are flexible.

Want to know if you are flexible? Sit on the floor with your legs stretched out together in front of you. Bend forward and touch your toes. Do not bend or lift your legs. Can you do it? If so, your back and leg muscles are flexible.

People who are in good shape have strong hearts and lungs. They can work hard without getting tired. They can also bend and stretch without hurting their muscles. They have the energy they need for the whole day!

CHAPTER THREE

How Can
You Get Fit?

The best way to get fit is to get moving! Activity is an important part

of fitness. Everyone needs to do aerobic activities two or three days a

week. Each activity should last at least 30 minutes. Walking to the

library, riding a bike, or playing tag with a group of friends are all

great ways to get

aerobic exercise.

You should warm

up and stretch out

before you start an

activity. If you are

playing a game that

involves running, you

You can aerobic exercise just by playing a game of tag.

There are many ways to warm up before you exercise. The important thing it to stretch those muscles!

can walk around slowly to warm up.

Jumping in place four or five times is another

way to get your muscles moving. You can also try bending over to

touch your toes or lifting your knees to your chest. These exercises

help stretch your muscles.

After exercising, you should cool down. This helps your heart

rate and breathing return to a normal pace. Slowly walking around

In-line skating is an easy way to keep your leg muscles strong.

is an easy way to do this. Stretching your muscles again is

important, too.

Everyone needs to do activities that will strengthen their

muscles. It's easy to keep your legs strong by walking, running,

or even in-line skating. It takes more planning to keep your arms,

back, and stomach muscles strong. Exercises such as sit-ups, push-

ups, or lifting small weights can help with these.

Lots of everyday activities can help build strong muscles. Carrying groceries from the car helps build arm muscles. So does rowing a boat when you go fishing. Gardening and raking are other good ways to build muscles in the upper body.

No matter what the activity, everyone needs to drink plenty of water. You should drink water before, during, and after your exercises. Your body needs water even when you are not thirsty. Most of us need six glasses of water a day. If the weather is hot, you need to drink even more.

Be sure you get plenty of water before, during, and after your activities.

CHAPTER FOUR

WHY DOES FOOD MATTER?

Balancing exercise with the right amounts and types of food is important. The body uses food as fuel when it is active. Food that is not used is stored as fat. Some fat is good for your body. But overeating and not getting enough exercise can add too much fat to your body.

Exercise alone can't keep you physically fit. You need to eat well, too.

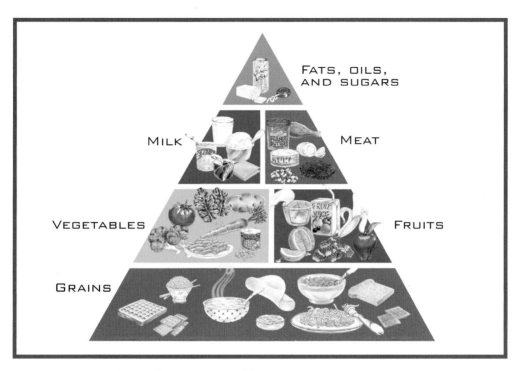

The Food Guide Pyramid helps you figure out what kinds of food you should eat and how much to eat every day.

So what types of food does the body need to stay fit? The Food Guide Pyramid divides food into five main groups. You need to eat the most of the foods that are found at the bottom of the pyramid. You only need a few servings of the foods at the top.

At the bottom are foods made from grains. They include bread, cereal, rice, and pasta. These foods give your body energy.

Eating plenty of fruits and vegetables each day helps your body fight diseases.

Next are the fruit and vegetable groups. These foods contain vitamins (VI-ta-mens) that our bodies need to prevent diseases. Did you know that many **athletes** eat bananas to keep their muscles from cramping?

On top of those groups are the milk and meat groups. These foods come mainly from animals, like fish, chicken, and cattle. Foods in this group contain calcium and protein (PRO-teen). Your body uses calcium to build strong bones and teeth. Protein is used to help muscles grow.

At the top of the pyramid are foods made from fats, oils, and sugars. Candy bars and cookies are examples of this group. Our bodies need very little of these foods each day.

Those cookies do taste good, but to stay healthy, your body should not have too many!

CHAPTER FIVE

WHY BE ACTIVE?

The ancient Greeks were some of the first people to recognize the importance of exercise for the body. At first, they trained their young men to be athletes so they would be good in war. Sports like **archery** and **wrestling** helped them develop the skills they needed for battle.

Soon, Greek doctors saw that physical activity helped make the human body healthy. One doctor

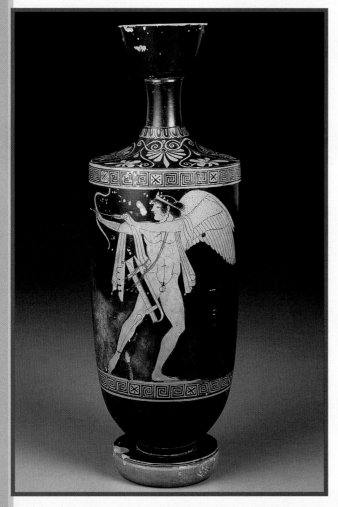

Paintings on vases by the ancient Greeks showed how they used archery to stay fit for battle.

wrote that "everyone, even infants" needed exercise. Centuries later, in the 1700s, an Italian doctor noticed that workers who sat in chairs all day were not as healthy as those who moved around at work. He told the "chair-workers" to exercise on their days off.

The idea that physical fitness could help prevent

The London Bus Driver Study

Doctors in London did an interesting study about 50 years ago. They studied workers on London's double-decker buses. These buses have upstairs and downstairs seating areas. The drivers sat at the front and drove the buses for several hours at a time. But the conductors walked the aisles collecting tickets. They also climbed up and down the stairs many times each hour.

The doctors studied the health of the drivers and the conductors. Which group was the most physically fit? Doctors found that the conductors had less heart disease than the drivers did. They also had fewer heart attacks. Including physical activity in your daily life can make a big difference!

disease became popular in the United States in the 1800s. Several books were written to teach parents and teachers about exercise. Children were taught to do calisthenics (cal-is-THEN-icks) in school. These were exercises that built strong muscles.

Today, one out of five children is overweight. This is a new health problem. Fewer children were overweight 20 years ago. Children who are overweight often are not active or do not eat the right foods.

Children started learning calisthenics in school in the 1800s.
This was an early version of gym class!

Obese adults often suffer from heart disease, strokes, diabetes, or high blood pressure.

Overweight children may grow up to be **obese** adults. Obesity can cause heart disease and diabetes. It can also lead to strokes and high blood pressure. Doctors think that children who are active and fit are more likely to stay active as adults. Activity can prevent these diseases from developing.

Yoga can be a relaxing and fun way to get exercise

Exercise is a good way to relax and to reduce stress. By reducing stress, you can also prevent disease. **Yoga** is a great way to relax. It helps you stretch and strengthen your muscles, too. So do other sports, such as tae kwon do and karate. Ballet is another activity that requires strength and flexibility.

Should you ever stop exercising? Doctors say no. Even older adults who use walkers or wheelchairs should do simple exercises. The activity will help them feel better and keep their muscles from getting stiff. They can also develop better balance with these exercises. That can keep them from falling.

Many senior citizens continue to exercise to keep in good shape. This man even competes in races!

CHAPTER SIX

How Can
You Stay Active?

Has your mother ever said you need to get outside and move

around? That is because getting exercise is a great way to gain energy.

Moving your muscles makes your heart push more oxygen and

nutrients through your body. Suddenly you have more energy.

Just getting outside and moving around for a while
can give you energy and make you feel better.

The same thing can happen in the classroom. You might have been sitting at your desk for a long time, reading or taking a test. You feel stiff and

Sitting at your desk at school all day can make you feel tired. Get up and get active!

tired. Standing by your desk and stretching or running a few laps around the gym can make a big difference. The extra oxygen in your body will help you think more clearly when you come back to your desk.

Do you know what double Dutch is? Or the swing kick and toe-to-toe? These are different ways to jump rope. Schools across the United States and Canada have formed jump-roping clubs as a fun

way to get students active. Maybe you can start a club at your school!

It is fun to do activities with other people. But what can you do

after school if you do not have anyone to play with? Being active is

Double Dutch is a great way to stay physically fit, for fun or in contests.

better than watching TV. Try practicing some new skills. Get a basketball and see how long you can dribble it without missing. Grab your tennis racquet and practice hitting a ball against a brick wall. Your friends will be surprised at how good you are the next time you play with them. How did you stay active today?

Get Moving!

Need some ideas? Here are some ways that you can get moving.

- ▸ If possible, walk places with your friends instead of getting a ride.

- ▸ Count how many times you can jump rope without missing.

- ▸ Shoot baskets with a friend.

- ▸ Turn on music and dance.

- ▸ Wash your parents' car.

- ▸ Strap on your helmet and ride your bike with a friend.

- ▸ Go for a walk with your family after dinner.

- ▸ Sweep an older neighbor's sidewalk.

- ▸ Rake the leaves and then jump into the pile.

- ▸ See how long you can keep a balloon in the air without letting it hit the floor.

- ▸ Take your dog for a walk. He needs to stay active, too!

Glossary

archery (AR-chuh-ree) Archery is the sport of shooting with a bow and arrow.

athlete (ATH-leet) An athlete is someone who competes in sports.

nutrients (NOO-tree-uhnts) Nutrients are the things found in foods needed for life and health.

obese (oh-BEESS) Someone who is obese is very overweight. Doctors use this word to describe people who are more than 20 percent heavier than they should be.

wrestling (RESS-ling) Wrestling is a contest between two people who try to throw each other down using their hands.

yoga (YOH-guh) Yoga is a tradition of exercises to develop the body and the mind.

Questions and Answers about Physical Fitness

How active do I need to be each day? Everyone needs at least 30 minutes of activity daily. This should be both aerobic and strengthening exercises.

What are some examples of aerobic activities? An aerobic activity makes your body use more oxygen. It makes your heart beat faster and your lungs breathe harder. Activities that include walking, running, biking, swimming, or jumping are all good aerobic activities.

How much aerobic exercise do I need? You should be aerobically active two or three times a week.

What other kinds of exercise do I need? You should do exercises that strengthen your muscles two or three times a week. You also need to stretch your muscles before and after every workout.

Did You Know?

▶ When you exercise, your brain releases chemicals called endorphins. They give you a happy feeling.

▶ President Dwight Eisenhower created the President's Council on Youth Fitness in 1956. Today, the council is called the President's Council on Physical Fitness and Sports. Its job is to encourage all Americans to be active and fit.

▶ If the average American eats 100 calories a day more than he needs, he will gain about 10 pounds in a year.

▶ Only 29 percent of children attend daily physical education classes in school. That is about 1 out of every 3 children.

▶ Recent studies have shown that vigorous exercise in childhood can reduce cholesterol levels and risk of heart disease in adulthood.

▶ Less than half of the children in the United States engage in activities that are vigorous enough to reduce heart disease risks or to have long-term health benefits.

▶ One quarter of children in the United States do no vigorous activities of any kind.

▶ Rigorous exercise can reduce stress and promote good mental health.

How to Learn More about Physical Fitness

At the Library: Nonfiction

Green, Jen. *Muscles.* Brookfield, Conn.: Copper Beech Books, 2003.

Koch, Isabelle. *Like a Fish in Water: Yoga for Children.*
Rochester, Vt.: Inner Traditions, 1999.

Simon, Seymour. *Muscles: Our Muscular System.*
New York: Morrow Junior Books, 1998.

Stewart, Mary, Kathy Phillips, and Sandra Lousada. *Yoga for Children.*
New York: Simon & Schuster, 1992.

At the Library: Fiction

Chang, Cindy, and Valerie Costantino (illustrator). *Jump! Jump!*
Los Angeles: Price Stern Sloan, 1996.

de Brunhoff, Laurent. *Babar's Yoga for Elephants.*
New York: Harry N. Abrams, 2002.

On the Web

Visit our home page for lots of links about exercise:
http://www.childsworld.com/links.html

Note to Parents, Teachers, and Librarians: We routinely verify our
Web links to make sure they're safe, active sites—so encourage your
readers to check them out!

Through the Mail or by Phone

Wheelchair Sports USA
3595 East Fountain Boulevard, #L-1
Colorado Springs, CO 80910
719/574-1150

U.S. Olympic Committee/Disabled Sports Services
One Olympic Plaza
Colorado Springs, CO 80909
719/578-4818

President's Council on Physical Fitness and Sports
Department W
200 Independence Avenue, S.W.
Room 738-H
Washington, DC 20201-0004
202/690-9000

Yoga is good both for your mind and for your body.

Index

About the Author

Shirley Wimbish Gray has been a writer and educator for more than 25 years and has published more than a dozen nonfiction books for children. She also coordinates cancer education programs at the University of Arkansas for Medical Sciences and consults as a writer with scientists and physicians. She lives with her husband and two sons in Little Rock, Arkansas.